10 May 1991

To Bob
my Beloved Son
The Sky is the limit
If you Choose
Dad

THE
WARBIRDS

THE
WARBIRDS

Rick Ruhman

MALLARD
PRESS

TABLE OF CONTENTS

ACKNOWLEDGEMENTS

Thanks to all the dedicated people who contribute in so many ways to the fine air shows and races around the country. Your organizational skills and concerns make it possible for all of us, of different generations and backgrounds, to enjoy, experience, appreciate and participate in the world of flight.

Many thanks to the air-to-air photo mission pilots: Al Goss, John Martin, Bill Porter, Ray Stallins, Bob Stickle, 'Stoney' Stonich and Eddie Van Fossen.

Special thanks to Bill Yenne for his expertise and putting this all together, to Randy Goss for help with the photo captions, to John and Barbara Ruhman for having and nurturing a young artist and to my wife, Denise, for always believing in my work.

All photographs are © 1990 by Rick Ruhman and may not be reproduced outside this book without his written permission.

Edited and designed by Bill Yenne

Page 1: It is exciting to see a formation flight of B-17s, an occurrence that is now quite rare, in contrast to the wartime days of 'thousand plane' raids. In formation are *Sentimental Journey* and David Tallichet's B-17G (this converted to B-17F configuration) at the 50th anniversary of the Flying Fortress at Seattle's Boeing Field in 1985.

Pages 2–3: Sundown at the Gathering of the Warbirds in Madera, California, as light reflects off *Miss Torque*, a P-51 Mustang owned by Robb Satterfield. The P-51 from Ed Maloney's Planes of Fame Museum rests in the background.

DEDICATION

To the pilots, the builders, the crews and their machines.

Ray 'Mac' McClain (*above left*) was the only pilot on the racing circuit to win the National Championship Race in both the T-6 and Unlimited racing classes. In 1972 he won the T-6 Championship flying Number 25, *Miss Eufaula*, an AT-6C. In 1980 he won the Unlimited Championship in the modified P-51D Mustang pictured here. Number 69, *Jeannie*, set a speed record of 433.01 mph, and has the longest racing career of any Mustang in history.

With McClain in this 1980 photo is Dave Zeuschel, who was already well known as a builder of fine drag racing engines when he turned his considerable talents to air racing in the mid-1960s.

Jeannie began her career in the late 1940s as Number 77, *The Galloping Ghost*, with either Steve Beville or Bruce

Raymond at the controls. In the late 1960s she was raced as Number 69, *Miss Candace*, with Cliff Cummins as pilot. *Jeannie* almost didn't make it to the 1980 Gold Race that she ultimately won. Dave Zeuschel had to make a forced landing, resulting in heavy damage to the airplane. Typical of any bellied-in Mustang, the prop and nose were ruined and the belly scoop flattened. Through a monumental effort—with less than a week to accomplish the task—the racing team rebuilt *Jeannie*. McClain was able to fly into the traffic pattern at Reno with just *one minute* to spare before the Wednesday noon arrival deadline.

McClain and Zeuschel, along with *Jeannie*, were members of the Sanders Truckline Racing Team, owned by Wiley Sanders.

Above: A red Fokker Dr-1 'dreidecker' triplane replica taken at the Antique Fly-In at Watsonville, California. Designed by Anthony Herman 'Tony' Fokker, the 'Flying Dutchman,' the original Dr-1 entered service with the German Imperial Air Force in 1917. The infamous Baron Manfred von Richthofen, the 'Red Baron,' achieved 80 victories over Allied machines in his bright red Dr-1 before he was shot down on 21 April 1918. Today, Dr-1s exist only in replica form. Many pilots have described the Dr-1, and the replicas thereof, as one of the worst aircraft to fly. Virtually everyone who flies one, or builds the replica, comes to not treat it lightly because it is such a dangerous machine, a reputation it gained in World War I when it was known to break apart in midair. It's amazing that the Red Baron ever garnered *any* victories in a Dr-1!

Although the Fokker triplane was credited with a great number of kills during World War I, history has looked at it as a fiasco. Several replicas have also been responsible for deaths and injuries of their own pilots, but they sure look pretty!

Note the ax handle on each wingtip, used here in lieu of stock, formed pieces of S-curved wood, as wingtip skids. The authentic skid was of the same general shape, but not quite as thick as an ax handle, and actually a little bit closer to the wingtip.

Right: The Stearman N2S Kaydett, the Navy version of the Army's great PT-17 Kaydett primary trainer, was known as the Yellow Peril because of its vivid color and the youth and awkwardness of its would-be pilots. With its narrow and short-coupled landing gear, the Stearman is a real handful for the novice pilot, hence the old quote: 'There are two kinds of pilots; those that have ground looped a Stearman and those that will.'

Many of the Stearman Kaydetts on the Warbird circuit, whether in Navy N2S or Army PT-17 markings, are former cropdusters. For forty years, the original surplus N2Ss and PT-17s were modified with hoppers, spraying equipment, different landing gear and larger engines. Because they were used for agricultural and commercial services, many relics could be found by the side of the road or in old barns. Many people have purchased and refurbished these aircraft for the Warbird circuit.

Many of the paint schemes seen on Stearmans today don't always show their specific former military livery. A PT-17, originally painted in Army markings, may now be outfitted in N2S Navy colors, and vice versa.

Above: A group shot of Stearman Kaydett biplanes, seen here in a classic air show formation pass. The plane at the *top* of the picture sports US Navy N2S markings, while the *middle* plane has civilian markings.

Left: A North American BT-13 basic trainer, silhouetted against a sunset at Hamilton Field in Marin County, California. In US Army service in the early 1940s, the BT-13 *basic* trainer was used after the Stearman PT-17 *primary* trainer and before the North American AT-6 Texan, which was an *advanced* trainer. Although similar in some ways to the later AT-6, the BT-13 had a fixed landing gear, rather than the retractable system found on the AT-6. This led to some problems for trainees, who occasionally forgot to either raise or lower the gear after they made the transition from the BT-13 to the AT-6. The BT-13 had a Pratt & Whitney R985 engine, which produced 450 hp, while the AT-6 had a Pratt & Whitney R1340, which produced 600 hp.

Below: A Waco Model UPF7 biplane, with colorful Bicentennial markings, taken in 1976 at Watsonville, California. In service as a primary trainer with the US Army Air Corps in 1939, the UPF7 flew under the designation PT-14. The Army itself had only 14 such aircraft, but many were used by the government's Civilian Pilot Training Program (CPTP). Note the attractive stars and bars motif in front, which is definitely *not* a stock military cowling!

Above: An air-to-air formation shot taken at the Madera Gathering of the Warbirds. In the lead is Arvin Pliss, forming up on the photo plane in his SNJ, while off his right wing is John Martin in *Old Boog 979*. SNJ was the US Navy's designation for the same aircraft that was designated AT-6 in US Army nomenclature. When the US Army Air Forces became the US Air Force in 1947, the AT-6s became simply T-6s.

Martin, who had a smoke system installed in his plane, enjoyed playing a practical joke on people who had never flown in a Warbird before. At take-off he would turn the smoke on, then roll the T-6 to the right so that the smoke would completely cover the canopy. Of course, the novice flier in the back would be thrown into a panic. The first time this author rode with Martin and smoke began to cover the plane, Martin asked worriedly, 'Gee, what's all that smoke?'

'I think it's that smoke oil you injected into the stack to your smoke system,' came the reply.

'Aw, you're no fun at all!' Martin complained.

Right: Cropduster pilot Jerry McDonald in *Big Red*, seen here in its 1981–1988 race paint. The former was the year that marked the return of T-6 racing at Reno after a two-year hiatus. The stock T-6 Racing Class is very competitive, and a former champion may end up in the slower Silver Race the very next year.

Above: A close-up of Charlie Beck, a former P-51 Mustang pilot during World War II, flying *Honest Entry*. Beck is a long-time racer at the Reno Air Races, flying both P-51s and T-6s. Because of some controversy surrounding other 'stock' T-6 components and racing practices, Beck renamed his 'honest' plane (the former *California Medfly*) as *Honest Entry* in 1982. The humorous artwork on the fuselage is from the talented hand of Charlie's wife, Pat, a well-known Southern California artist.

Above: Three T-6s coming in, with Charlie Beck in *Honest Entry* in the lead. Above him is Jim Good in *The Wildcatter*, and last is Jim Mott, in Number 42. It is rare to see Mott, who was having a tough race, coming in third.

Right: Close in the *foreground* is *The Wildcatter*, a T-6 flown by Jim Good from Casper, Wyoming. In the *background*, the black Number 42 is Jim Mott's *Mis-Chief*. It is unusual to see Mott *following* anyone!

Overleaf: Jim Mott's Number 42, *Mis-Chief*. His glossy black T-6 racer sports a gold foil 'Chief' symbol, reflecting his ancestry. Mott, a well-known, major competitor, was a first place winner at the Mojave T-6 Races. He is known to fly high on the course above the other racers. Waiting for the last lap, he dives, trading altitude for air speed, and often nips someone out at the home pylon finish line.

Mott recently sold this aircraft to compete in the Unlimited Class, using Sea Fury Number 42 with a gigantic Bristol Centaurus engine attached to it.

Above: North American T-6s at the start of the Silver Race at the Reno Championship Air Races in 1989. From *left to right* the aircraft are: Bud Granley, flying the white and cordovan-colored *Lickety Split*, and John Luther in Number 20. In dead center is Charles Hutchins in Number 1, *Silver Baby*. On top is David Bruce in Number 4, *Slo Thunder*, and to the far right is Jim Good in Number 77, *The Wildcatter*. Hutchins, also the winner of the 1988 Silver Race, later went on to win this race, thus racking up back-to-back victories, a highly unusual feat in the tight competition of T-6 air racing.

Left: The aircraft on the *left* is *Big Red*, flown by Jerry McDonald, while on the *right* is Number 9, *Lickety Split*, an SNJ-5 flown by Bud Granley, seen here competing in the Reno Silver Race. Both aircraft are former Gold Race champions in the T-6 racing class. *Lickety Split*—then Number 9, *Gotcha*—was piloted to its Gold Race victory in 1974 by Pat Palmer at 211.35 mph. Number 9 was also raced by Bob Heale.

Granley also raced Mustangs and Texans at Reno, and for a number of years he piloted *Miss America*, a very famous P-51 Mustang, known by its unique red, white and blue coloring and starred paint scheme. Nicknamed '*Miss A*,' *Miss America* has also been raced by Howie Keefe.

Facing page: Bob Heale, in Number 9, *Lickety Split*, taking a brief respite from the sweltering sun at Reno in 1987. The heat of 1987 contrasts to the snow squalls that often hit Reno in September.

Above: *Warlock*, owned by cropduster Al Goss of Bakersfield, California. Number 75 is known for being a real crowd favorite wherever she appears. The author is proud to be one of the *Warlock* Air Racing Team's original crew members. *Warlock* is an SNJ-6, the Navy equivalent of the Army AT-6 and Air Force T-6 designation. It is one of the fastest T-6 Class aircraft in the world today.

Warlock, which has been a main competitor in Reno since 1981, is known for being exceptionally clean and as one of the shiniest aircraft on the field.

Note the shape of the left and right wings. One is much wider and fatter than the other due to the tremendous twisting forces the plane is subjected to, such as air mass and the torque of the propeller. Also note, on the right side of the picture, how the tip of the left horizontal stabilizer is dipped down, compared to the right side, again, due to air stress.

The T-6 Class of air racers is a stock class, one of the tightest of racing classes. Because they are required to be stock, the aircraft are very evenly matched.

Unlike most T-6 crews, the Unlimited Class crews often work well into the night on their complex 'big iron' racers. For a few seasons, though, the *Warlock* crew found themselves in the same late night work schedule. Al Goss later revealed his appreciation and sense of humor (he worked

late too) when he awarded each crew member a plaque which read 'Best "Unlimited" T-6 Crew.'

Since its racing debut in 1981, *Warlock* has become one of the toughest competitors in T-6 Class racing and is one of the fastest of its type in the world.   Compare the widths of the wings and horizontal stabilizer to get an idea of the tremendous forces working on this airframe and the stamina required to race it.

The T-6 Racing Class is known for the closest, most competitive and most evenly matched racing there is. Because it is a stock racing class, competitors are only allowed to 'clean up' the aircraft for better aerodynamic flow.

At the Championship Gold Race level, the Texans' top air speeds may be within two to three mph of each other, and one or two wide pylon turns can cost a pilot the race. This, combined with their loud roar (the prop tips go supersonic at maximum power), always makes for crowd-pleasing competition.

Facing page: A breathtaking view of *Warlock* taken from Reno's Pylon Two as Al Goss racks it over in one of his typical low, tight, smooth turns. Goss is known to make up valuable time and distance on virtually every turn, much to the chagrin of a pilot in the lead who suddenly finds himself looking at Al's 'tail feathers.'

These pages: Al Goss's *Warlock* enroute to the 1989 Hamilton Field Air Show, seen here flying over the San Francisco Bay. The author took this shot while riding with Eddie Van Fossen in 'the fastest T-6 on the planet.' Van Fossen came in second at the Reno Air Races three months later, but he still holds the record for highest qualifying speed and highest race speed. The man in the back seat is Philip Makanna, the well-known aviation photographer.

Above: This close-up of Al Goss in *Warlock* shows a number of the minor modifications that are allowed in the 'stock' T-6 racing class. Note the 'gear seals'—the rubber panels with silver rivets in the wheel wells. These keep air flow out of the wheel wells, which could cost a racer several mph. The canopy glass is all flush fit instead of recessed the usual 1/4 inch, and the side panels and leading edges of the wings have been smoothed and streamlined for a better air flow and improved performance. These modifications may seem minor, but are expensive, and they can make all the difference in a race. With a talented, experienced pilot, a hard-working crew and a strong, smooth-running engine in a cleaned up air frame, a racer has a good shot at the Gold.

Right: *Warlock* in the pits at Reno with its colors unfurled, waving above. Flying a standard, or 'colors,' is an ancient military tradition that the *Warlock* Race Team helped rekindle in the T-6 group, and many flags can now be seen in the pit area. The *Warlock* Racing Team's official 'camp mom,' Lola Worth, spent many hours designing, hand stitching and assembling flags for *Warlock*, as well as for a number of other racers.

Above: *Warlock* arriving at Madera, California. Al's hand is extended to ask, 'Where do I park this thing?' After landing, Al will enjoy an ice-cold Dr Pepper, his drink of choice.

These pages: The Lockheed P-38 Lightning known as *White Lightnin'*, flown by the great Lefty Gardner, a crop-duster pilot from Mercedes, Texas. This aircraft has its original Confederate Air Force 'Ghost Squadron' civilian paint scheme, a rare sight now that most pilots are going back to authentic World War II colors and markings.

Lefty is known for his low, tight pylon turns at the races and his outstanding aerobatic acts at air shows nation-wide. Although the race speed of Lefty's P-38—one of the rarest aircraft on the air show circuit—is not very competitive, he more than makes up for it with his skillful, popular flying displays. Like the P-51D *Jeannie*, this P-38 started racing in the late 1940s.

Above: Known as *Mr Awesome*, this is a Russian Yakovlev Yak-11 dating from the mid- to late 1940s. *Mr Awesome* has, however, been dramatically altered for air racing. Its cockpit area has been pushed back, and it has a totally different tail. Its engine, a turbo-compound R3350, is enormous in contrast to its lighter airframe. This appears to be the future trend in racing aircraft. After this photo was taken in 1988, a new propeller and spinner, as well as the tail section from a T-33 jet, were added.

Aircraft types originating in the Soviet Union can be obtained when governments—such as Pakistan and India—sell off their long-mothballed fleets. Most of these aircraft eventually find their way to the air racing and Warbird circuit in the United States, because that is where the money exists to buy and restore them.

Left: Bob Yancy's Yak-11 Number 101 is similar to *Mr Awesome* (*above*), but has a smaller engine. Howie Keefe's famous P-51D, *Miss America*, is in the background. Bob Yancy has been racing this aircraft since 1987, and in 1989 he worked his way to a showing in the Gold Race.

Before he started racing his Yak, Bob flew his Corsair *Old Blue*. He decided that it wasn't quite fast enough, so he bought this Russian aircraft from Egypt in 1986. He took the engine, and basically everything else from the firewall forward, out of his Corsair and put it on the Yak. It is powered by an R2800 radial engine, which is also found on Grumman Hellcats, Bearcats and a number of other aircraft. The spinner is from a Britannia airliner and the prop blades are from a North American T-28 trainer.

An amusing controversy surrounding this aircraft is its bright, chartreuse green trim. For the most part, however, it has a beautiful natural metal finish. Originally, Yaks were fabric-covered from the cockpit back, but the ones on the racing circuit have all been metalized to strengthen them. Only the undercarriage, the wings and a little bit of the tail are original—nearly everything else has been fabricated.

Overleaf: Tom Camp's Curtiss P-40 Warhawk at the Madera Gathering of the Warbirds. The classic 'shark mouth' was originally made famous on the P-40s of General Claire Chennault's American Volunteer Group (AVG)—the famed 'Flying Tigers' who went to China to help the Chinese fight the Japanese in the year before the United States entered World War II. When the United States entered the war in December 1941, Chennault's Flying Tigers became the China Air Task Force of the Tenth US Army Air Force, and in March 1943 they became the Fourteenth US Army Air Force. Note the underside where the red late afternoon sunlight has changed its normal light blue color to purple.

Left and above: Produced at a cost of $63,100 in 1944, this Grumman F6F-5 Hellcat was newly restored in 1989 at a cost reported to be 15 times that of the original price tag. It carries the markings of the famous US Navy ace Alexander Vraciu, who came over from Danville, California to see this aircraft.

The Hellcat was instrumental in changing the course of the war in the Pacific during World War II. A descendant of the Grumman F4F Wildcat, the Hellcats first saw action in August 1943 at Marcus Island in the Pacific theater. The highlight of the F6F's career came in June 1944, on the first day of the Battle of the Philippine Sea, aka 'Marianas Turkey Shoot,' when Hellcats completely smashed the Japanese attack, claiming most of the 300 planes lost by the enemy. Almost 75 percent of the US Navy's air-to-air victories during the war were scored by Hellcats, with an incredible kill ratio of 19 to one.

Today, however, it is rare to see one on the air show circuit, as only a handful are still in existence. After the war most Hellcats, like most P-38s and many Mustangs, were flown directly to smelters to be broken up and melted down en masse.

Above: These men are 'swinging the compass,' or setting up the compass for a perfect north-south-east-west reading. The man standing out front and the man inside are in radio contact with each other. The person on the side of the aircraft is being told to swing the tail over just another fraction of an inch, because aligning the compass is very critical, especially when doing navigation over land.

Rare Bear
AIRCRAFT
CYLINDER
&TURBINE
CHAMPION
PENNZOIL
Lyle Shelton

14P
14
P

Above: Lyle Shelton's 1988 and 1989 world champion Bearcat at the 1989 Reno Air Races. Earlier in 1989, Shelton broke the world speed record for propeller-driven aircraft in this plane, with 528 mph. It is now regarded as the fastest propeller-driven aircraft in history.

Left: Howard Pardue's XF8F-1, one of the first 23 pre-production Bearcats produced in 1945, and a very rare aircraft indeed. This picture is an in-flight photo of the 'Cat going around the pylons at Reno. Pardue, who hails from Breckinridge, Texas, has his own 'air force' of a Vought F4U Corsair, a Grumman F4F Wildcat, and a T-6 Texan, among others. He has been racing Number 14 for a number of years. It carries his initial 'P' on its tail.

Above: John Herlihy's Grumman F8F Bearcat outlined against the setting sun at Madera, California. In the background is a C-46 Curtiss Commando. The Bearcat's folded wings indicate that it was once a Navy carrier-based aircraft. The Bearcat has one of the toughest undercarriages of any flying machine ever designed. Note the large, paddle-bladed props. In its time, it was designed to have the biggest engine attached to the smallest, most tapered fuselage that could be designed. Although the F8F was a World War II-era design, it did not enter service until just after the war ended.

Right: An early morning view of John Herlihy's Grumman F8F Bearcat at Madera.

A sunset shot at the Madera Gathering of the Warbirds. In the *foreground* is the General Motors TBM Avenger owned by Bill Porter of Sacramento, California. The Avenger was originally designed by Grumman as TBF, but there are probably no authentic Grumman-built TBF Avengers still flying. The TBM was produced in greater numbers. There were a total of 2295 TBFs built, compared to 2889 TBMs.

Right: General Motors TBM Avenger, owned by Gordon Plaskett, as seen at the Gathering of the Warbirds in Madera, California.

Above: A nicely restored General Motors-built TBM Avenger belonging to Bill Porter of Sacramento, California. The Avenger was originally designed by Grumman as the TBF, but most of them were built by General Motors under the TBM designation. A veteran of World War II action, this Avenger has five torpedo marks, three rising suns and 15 bomb markings on the side, which belong to the owner and are not this *specific* aircraft's original markings. Near the windscreen is an original World War II aerial movie camera. It also carries underwing bombs and underwing rockets, which is unusual, because they more typically carried a single torpedo in an internal bay.

One time, Porter was at work on his gun turret and jokingly told the author that if he happened to have a Sperry Ball Turret manual on him, it would be helpful. A week later, the author's wife, Denise, found one at a flea market for 50 cents.

These pages: A two-seater, or 'two-holer,' this Mark IX Supermarine Spitfire dual control trainer is a very unusual aircraft rarely seen in the United States, or anywhere. Photographed here at the Gathering of the Warbirds in Madera, California, this Spitfire was once owned by Woody Woods and later by Bill Greenwood. Note the large wing cannon. Jack Erickson of Central Point, Oregon owns the first two-seat Supermarine Spitfire ever built, a Mark VIII.

Left: A Hispano Ha-1112, owned by Bubba Beale, which is basically a Spanish-built version of the German Messerschmitt Bf-109G-6, with a Rolls Royce Merlin engine. This Ha-1112 is painted in an approximation of World War II German Luftwaffe markings. From the firewall rearward, this aircraft could be a stock 1943 Messerschmitt Bf-109G 'Gustav.' The original Bf-109G had a Damlier-Benz DB-601 engine, an inverted V-12, in which the stacks were much lower, as compared to those of the Merlin seen here. The stock Messerschmitt Bf-109 also had a large, three-bladed paddle prop.

In 1981, this Ha-1112 ground-looped and tore most of its undercarriage off, a common problem for war-era Bf-109s, which encountered most of their handling difficulties landing and taking off. This problem was due to its very weak, narrow undercarriage. This particular Hispano was later given to Ed Maloney at the Planes of Fame Museum in Chino, California, and in 1989 it underwent a complete restoration and was given a more authentic Bf-109-type engine cowling.

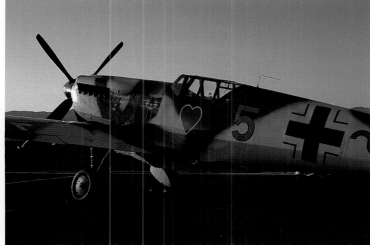

Above: Late sunset shots of Bubba Beale's Hispano Ha-1112. The insignia on the side are those of the Jagdstaffelen (fighter squadrons) of the Luftwaffe Jagdgeschwader (Fighter Group) 54, aka Grunherz (Green Heart), which served on the Eastern Front during World War II. These insignia appeared on Bf-109E, Bf-109F and Bf-109G aircraft throughout the war, although it is unlikely that all three ever appeared simultaneously on the same operational aircraft.

Left: The Fieseler Fi-156 Storch (Stork) was designed in Germany in 1935 by Gerhard Fiesler. This aircraft has been restored to German markings as a medical aircraft. What is so amazing about this early STOL (short take-off and landing) aircraft is that it can fly at *very* low airspeeds. With any kind of head wind, it can take off and rise almost vertically, then come to a complete stop. With a substantial head wind, it will actually fly backward because of its many special, large lift devices. Its long, cross-braced landing gear can take hard landings well. The Fi-156 was made famous when used in the daring rescue of Benito Mussolini from the mountaintop fortress where he was being held by mutineers. Note the leading edge slats, various lift devices and flaps and extremely long, sprung undercarriage.

Above: A Messerschmitt Bf-108 aircraft, owned by Harold Kindsvater. Designed by Willy Messerschmitt in 1933 for the general aviation market, the four-seat Bf-108 was ahead of its time and very well received before the war. During the war, Bf-108s were used by the Luftwaffe in a utility role. Though it is quite unusual, the author has also seen this paint scheme on World War II-era Bf-109s. This aircraft is a real crowd-pleaser on the air show circuit because of its German origin.

Above: Designed by Messerschmitt as a follow-on to the Bf-108, the Bf-208 continued to be built after the war by Nord in France, using surplus German parts. Today, this Nord Bf-208 is owned by Harold Kindsvater. Note the difference in the nose configuration and landing gear from the Bf-108.

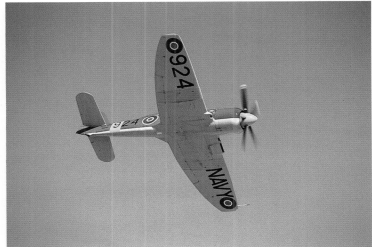

Above: Hawker Sea Fury, Number 924, owned by the Sanders family and flown here at Reno by Dennis Sanders.

Above: Lloyd Hamilton's Hawker Sea Fury Number 16, *Baby Gorilla*, taxies out at the Madera Gathering of the Warbirds. Most of the Sea Furies seen racing at Reno don't use the Bristol Centaurus sleeve-valve engine, which is a good, high-performance engine that fits well to the cowling. For the extra power they need to be competitive, the Bristol Centaurus is replaced with a Pratt & Whitney R4360 radial, which has four rows of seven cylinders—28 cylinders in all. One common problem with this engine is that the rear two banks of seven get overheated and may seize.

These engines do not have to be run very hard to produce excellent speeds, so pilots don't have to push them 'flat out' and risk losing control of their aircraft. In fact, the performance envelope of this engine really hasn't been reached yet. The R4360 engine is also in use in the Super Corsairs and Sea Furies that are currently on the racing circuit.

Left: Airline pilot Ellsworth Goetchell in his Hawker Sea Fury, Number 105 in Australian markings. Although very similar in appearance to Lloyd Hamilton's, this Sea Fury is painted in a lighter green and a darker gray.

This aircraft was raced in the 1960s by Tom Taylor, before being retired for a long time to undergo extensive restoration. Goetchell took seven years to complete this beautiful restoration.

Above: Jim Mott, a well-known T-6 racer, in his Sea Fury, Number 42, with a Bristol Centaurus engine and a large, oversized prop, taken from a Blackburn Beverly, a British transport aircraft.

This Sea Fury has a long racing history. It was raced cross-country and in pylon races by such notables as 1989 champion Lyle Shelton, Mike Carroll and Sherman Cooper. Carroll once gave it the wildest paint job it ever had. Overall it was bright yellow, with its entire nose covered with flames of purple, blue, red and orange, like those found on a hot rod. After Cooper had a landing accident in it, Jim Mott purchased and restored it to the condition seen here.

In the distant background on the right is Mott's former T-6 racer, Number 42, *Mis-Chief*.

Left: Frank, Dennis and Brian Sanders built this world champion air racer, *Dreadnaught*, with a huge Pratt & Whitney R4360 radial engine. It was named after the World War I class of British battleships that 'feared nothing.' This was the aircraft that brought 'round' engines back to Reno, where Mustangs, with their in-line engines, had dominated for many years. With Neil Anderson and Rick Brickert flying it, *Dreadnaught* broke all records, and its victories brought radial racing engines respectability. Not only beautiful to look at, *Dreadnaught* is still one of the world's fastest air racers.

Above: The late afternoon sun shows off the high gloss of English pilot/owner Rob Lamplough's Canadian-marked Hawker Sea Fury, which was restored by Frank Sanders.

These pages: A late September rain pelts Frank Sanders' stock Bristol Centaurus-powered Sea Fury, which sports a standard five-bladed prop.

Lloyd Hamilton's Sea Fury, *Furias*, with red cowling and Pratt & Whitney R4360 engine, stands in the background.

Above: *Little Demon*, a Republic P-47 Thunderbolt, owned by Ray Stutsman of Elkhart, Indiana, at the Madera Gathering of the Warbirds in the mid-1980s, when only a handful of Thunderbolts were still flying. Painted in Walter Beckham's markings, this aircraft is immaculate, inside and out. White cowlings were common to the 388th Fighter Squadron of the 365th Fighter Group of the Ninth US Army Air Force.

Left: A Republic P-47D restored by the Planes of Fame West Museum and owned by Bob Pond. The bubble canopy was an innovation introduced into mass production on the P-47D, and is in contrast to earlier Thunderbolts, in which the pilot's rear visibility was greatly obscured. Red cowlings were common to many Thunderbolt squadrons in the Ninth US Army Air Force during World War II.

Above and *right*: Bob Reiser's Bell P-63 King Cobra. Designed as a follow-on to Bell's unpopular P-39 Airacobra, today the King Cobra is a very rare aircraft.

Bob Reiser always enjoyed making a dramatic entrance at air shows with this bright red beauty by flying in like a comet at nearly 'warp' speed. He would bring it right down on the runway, and then pull straight up, almost vertically, until it would bleed off.

This aircraft was later owned by English Warbird collector Stephen Gray. Like the P-39, the P-63 had its engine in mid-fuselage, and that always gave pilots something to worry about. The engine is located just behind the pilot, so crash-landing can be dangerous. The drive shaft housing, which is right between the pilots legs, has to be fairly substantial to keep a broken drive shaft from injuring him.

Above: John Maloney flying *Super Corsair*, a Vought F4U-1, an early model 'birdcage' Corsair, converted into a racer by Ed Maloney and Steve Hinton of Fighter Rebuilders, which is part of the Planes of Fame Museum at Chino in Southern California. It is now powered by a huge Pratt & Whitney R4360 engine. During the Gold Race at Reno in 1985, in which it captured the Unlimited World Championship, it was competing against Neil Anderson in the Hawker Sea Fury *Dreadnaught*. Anderson, who was leading the race, received a reading from the ground that he had cylinder head temperature problems. He took a moment to check his gauge and 'cut the pylon' (cut inside the course just a hair), and this cost him a lap, making this F4U-1 the winner.

Right: Steve Rosenberg flying *Blue Max*, a Vought F4U Corsair which he co-owned with Bob Guilford, on an air-to-air mission over Yolo County, near Davis, California. Number 93 was a popular fixture on the air show circuit for many years.

Above: Steve Rosenberg taxies *Blue Max* out for a day's enjoyment. In this close-up view, the aircraft's split flaps are clearly visible. The flaps are split to accommodate the wings, which were designed to fold for storing the Corsair on the crowded hangar deck of an aircraft carrier.

Above: Two B-25 Mitchell bombers in formation. The plane on the *right* is *Dream Lover*, owned by Jim Ricketts of Stockton, California, a natural metal beauty. Note the gunpacks and gun nose. The other B-25, in Canadian markings, has its bomb bay open to drop watermelons in a mock bomb run on an improvised 'Officers' Club.'

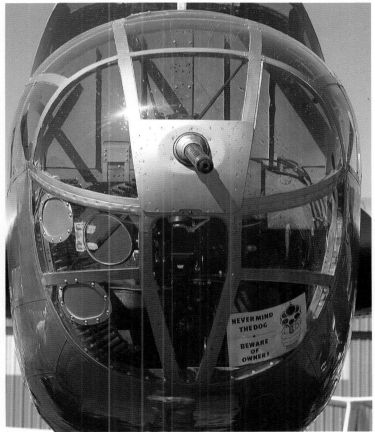

Above: The North American B-25 Mitchell bomber was made famous by General Jimmy Doolittle's daring raid on Japan on 18 April 1942. In this view, the 50 caliber machine gun pointing directly at the camera is underscored by a message that echoes that which was delivered to the Japanese warlords by Jimmy Doolittle. Note also the auxiliary gunports on the left hand side.

Left: This North American B-25 Mitchell is named for bandleader Glenn Miller's 1939 hit song. Later, US Army Air Forces Major Glenn Miller toured the world entertaining troops, until he was killed in an airplane crash in December 1944. *In the Mood* is seen here at the Madera Gathering of the Warbirds in 1984. Five B-25s came to this particular gathering, where they marked the 42nd anniversary of Doolittle's raid on Tokyo.

Left and above: *Dago Red*, the 1982 national champion and former world speed record holder at 15 kilometers, clocked at 517.079 mph, is a highly modified P-51 Mustang, with clipped wings, a clipped horizontal stabilizer and a reduced-size canopy. Built by Frank Taylor and Bill 'Tiger' DeStefani, *Dago Red* has been a main competitor in the Gold Races for many years. Taylor and DeStefani later sold this aircraft to well-known race pilot Alan Preston, and it is currently owned by David Price.

Above: *Merlin's Magic*, a beautiful, silver P-51D owned by Stu Eberhart, in the pits at Reno in 1989. Note the yellow rudder and post-World War II markings. The rudder is from 'pilot's pilot' Bob Hoover's Mustang, *Old Yeller*. After Eberhart had the trim tab blown off his own rudder, Hoover loaned Stu his so he could continue to race.

Overleaf: A close-up of two P-51 model Mustangs. *Miss Torque*, in the *background*, is owned by Robb Satterfield. In the *foreground* is Mike Clarke's *Unruly Julie*, an outstanding restoration with a brightly colored, checkerboard nose.

Above: A banked shot of a North American P-51D Mustang, Number 39, *The Healer*/'*Super K*'. It is owned by Joe Kasparoff and raced by Skip Holm. Back in the late 1960s, it was owned and raced by Burns Byrum, who also owned the P-51 called *Tangerine*.

Right: A close-up view of Joe Kasparoff's P-51D, *The Healer* (aka '*Super K*'), showing the aircraft's colors. This aircraft shines like a mirror. A North American T-28 Trojan can be seen in the background.

Below: *Georgia Mae* has a long race career. It was once raced as Number 17, *Escape I*, by Mac McClain and by Jack Sliker. It has since been owned by Wiley Sanders.

Above: An air-to-air view of three P-51 Mustangs forming up at Madera, California. The two with red noses and World War II-era US Army Air Forces markings belong to Dan Martin and Angelo Regina. The third aircraft, in postwar US Air Force/Air National Guard markings, belongs to Robb Satterfield. After 1947, US Air Force P-51s were redesignated as F-51s.

Right: Bill 'Tiger' DeStefani's stunning P-51 Mustang, *Strega* (which means 'witch' in Italian). DeStefani's 1987 world championship victory had a true storybook ending. Before race week began, Bill announced he would run hard in every heat, win them, set a new qualifying record and win the championship race—a tall order, considering the competition and stress on his aircraft. He and his crew did it all! In 1989 DeStefani came within a few seconds of capturing the title again, before having to pull out due to a blown water gasket.

This picture was taken at Hamilton Field at the first races to be held in the San Francisco Bay Area in over 30 years. Hamilton Field is a historic Air Force base which dates from the 1920s. DeStefani, landing after having been beaten by Lyle Shelton, waves his hand as if to say 'I don't know what happened!'

The canopy on *Strega* is a custom design that can be jettisoned by the pilot, if necessary. It has just enough room for the pilot and his helmet, providing a streamlined effect.

Above: A P-51D Mustang owned by Ted Contri of Reno, Nevada, taken at Watsonville, California in 1981. This aircraft is one of the few Mustangs on the circuit with a civilian paint scheme that hasn't been returned to the military markings that came into favor in the late 1970s.

Above: Two P-51s in a 1988 heat race. At the *top* is David Price in Mustang Number 49, a fairly stock P-51D. Note the long bubble canopy and stock wing length. *Below*, by comparison, is *Dago Red*, flown by Alan Preston, which has a tiny canopy, clipped wings and a clipped horizontal stabilizer.

Right: *Man o' War*, a P-51D Mustang owned by Elmer Ward, in World War II markings, as seen at Hamilton Field. The markings are those of Lt Col CH Kinnard, whose name is on the pilot's identification strip on the plane. The swastika kill-markings are authentic. Unique to this plane are the rearview mirrors, which are British in origin. Usually you see *one*, but this aircraft has *two* mirrors—one in each corner—a configuration often used by the British during World War II.

PILOT
LT. COL. C. H. KINNARD

Above: Bob Love's Mustang being readied for an early evening ride at Madera, with the chute thrown up on the wing. The six red stars date to Love's Korean War days, when he garnered victories against Chinese MiGs.

Left: One of the Warbird circuit's great Mustang pilots, the late Bob Love, flying *Jolly Roger*. Love was a fighter pilot in the Korean War, and was one of the most well-respected fliers on the Warbird circuit. When experienced high time pilots got together and he started talking, they'd all listen to Bob, one of the few times you could get them to listen. Bob would always talk about formation. He was known at air shows for his hair-raising rolls, just after take-off, in which he allowed only a minimum of clearance for the wing tips to go by the ground.

On the left side of the aircraft is the phrase *Illigitimatus Non Carborundum*, which is Latin for 'Don't let the bastards get you down.' Russ Francis, a pro football player with the San Francisco 49ers, later owned this airplane.

Back in the 1970s, this aircraft was raced with clipped wings and a small canopy as Number 97, *The Ooga-honk Special*. This photograph shows it after its restoration to a stylized World War II-era configuration.

Left: This view highlights the long nose on Bob Love's P-51 aircraft. Note the wing drop tank mounting points just outboard of the landing gear. This gear, which is quite wide, was standard to all Mustangs, and makes this high performance racing craft easier to land.

Right: A rear angle view of Clay Klabo's P-51D, *Fat Cat*.

Above: A line-up of five North American P-51 Mustangs, with a variety of configurations and color schemes.

Right: *Dago Red* at the end of a day's excitement, while crews finish up their work.

Above: A sleeping 'witch'—Bill DeStefani's 1987 champion *Strega* parked peacefully for the night.

Above: Crews of the Unlimiteds work far into the night. Here, a crew conducts an engine change on Jimmy Leeward's *Specter* at the Reno Air Races in 1983. Note the Rolls Royce Merlin engine in the foreground. Some of these engines cost $80,000 each, and some teams may use two or three engines during a single race week.

Facing page: The late Jim Orton flying the Confederate Air Force's B-17G, *Sentimental Journey*, during over a dozen consecutive buzz jobs at the Madera Gathering of the Warbirds.

Orton was also famous for showing off his famous one-wheel landing simulation (*center*), which he used to recreate a similar landing used by one of the B-17 that stumbled into Hickam Field on the morning of 7 December 1941 *during* the attack on Pearl Harbor, and that were set upon by the Japanese warplanes. Orton was able to come in, delicately touch down on one wheel and hold the plane in the same position the entire length of the runway.

Above: In a scene that could have taken place four decades earlier, Boeing's B-17F firebomber (*top*), is seen along with the B-17G *Sentimental Journey* (*left*).

Originally built for the USAAF, the top aircraft served with the US Forest Service for many years, dropping borate on forest fires, until Boeing bought it back in the 1980s. It has since been restored to its original World War II configuration. Providing escort for the bombers here, as they did in World War II, are (*left to right*) *Ho Hun*, a North American P-51D Mustang, owned by Bill Hane, and a Republic P-47 Thunderbolt, *Little Demon*, flown by Ray Stutsman.

Above: *Sentimental Journey*, one of the most beautifully restored Boeing B-17 Flying Fortress currently flying in the United States, which is operated by the Southern Arizona Wing of the Confederate Air Force. It is seen here at Boeing Field in Seattle in 1985 during the 50th anniversary celebration of the B-17 Flying Fortress. *Sentimental Journey* is a B-17G, the final production model, which is distinguished from earlier Flying Fortresses by its having a chin turret.

In the *foreground* (in the blue cap) is Edward S Michael of Fairfield, California, one of a handful of World War II veterans who received the Medal of Honor piloting a B-17. His last mission, on 11 April 1944, ended when he belly-landed his shot-up B-17 at the British air base near Grimsby, England.

Michael had been flying 'coffin corner' (the upper, outer element of the high squadron) when, 10 miles from Berlin, the squadron turned on their IP (initial point) of the mission, heading for Stettin, Germany. Suddenly, a wave of 130 German interceptors dropped down on their forma-

tion. A Bf-109G put four 20mm cannon rounds into the B-17, only to be shot down by the top turret gunner, Jewel Phillips.

One round came in just ahead of the windscreen and detonated against the control column, spewing schrapnel into Michael's left thigh, and causing severe damage to the controls and most of the instruments in the cockpit. Another round whistled in and detonated inside the top turret, seriously wounding Phillips and knocking out the turret. A third round exploded above the windshield, opaquing Michael's forward view. The most critical round exploded in the bomb bay, setting the plane's load of 42 100-pound incendiary bombs *on fire*. Michael in turn discovered that they were unable to jettison the load.

Michael ordered the crew to bail out of the badly damaged plane, but he, copilot Frank Westberg, top turret gunner Jewel Phillips and bombardier John Lieber remained. They flew for 20 minutes with the incendiaries burning, the casings melting on top of one another, but somehow they did not explode. At this point, Michael and

Lieber put a parachute on the badly wounded Phillips, placing the pull ring in his remaining good hand. Phillips bailed out, and miraculously landed next to a German field hospital, where he was given medical care. He was kept as a German prisoner of war for the rest of the war, but he survived and today lives in Louisiana.

One of the four hits had chopped the linkages on two of the the B-17's throttles. The plane endured several more fighter attacks, with Michael corkscrewing the aircraft through the clouds, trying to shake the fighters. Lieber, after trying everything he could, finally managed to jettison all but one of the burning incendiaries.

Entering the bomb bay without a parachute and without guide ropes, which had been burned away, he balanced on a very narrow catwalk with open air below him. Standing on one leg and kicking with the other, Lieber was finally able to knock the remaining bomb out of the bay.

With the use of only a handful of serviceable instruments, Michael, Westberg and Lieber hedge-hopped their way across Germany and into the Netherlands. Farmers on the ground, seeing their difficulty, waved their hats to get their attention and then pointed the direction to England with their hands and pitchforks. When they reached the English Channel, they spotted an English flotilla and thought to ditch nearby, but because the only thing the British would see in the dense fog was a large bomber looming overhead with its bomb bay doors flung open, they decided to press on.

Finally, they came to the British Royal Air Force base near Grimsby. After making one pass down the field, Michael belly-landed the plane on the grass, just off the main runway. In the process, the bomb bay doors and belly turret were ground off the plane, but Michael still made what the commanding officer of the base described with characteristic British understatement as 'the finest belly landing he had ever seen.' Michael was presented his Medal of Honor by President Franklin D Roosevelt.

Michael was not to set foot in a B-17 again until the day these pictures were taken, more than 40 years later.

INDEX

Facing page: A vertical formation of three P-51 Mustangs. On the *bottom* is Elmer Ward flying *Man o' War*, with *Unruly Julie*, owned by Mike Clarke of Arizona, flown by Jeff Ethell, *above*. The *top* Mustang, which sports postwar US Air Force/Air National Guard markings, belongs to Robb Satterfield. Note the wing tanks on these planes. Used during World War II to help extend the range of P-51s escorting bombers into the heart of the German Reich, wing tanks are hard to find these days. The P-51 escorts were able to penetrate deep into Germany on round-trip missions, with one group going in and another group meeting the bombers on their way out, thus providing protection to the bombers throughout their entire mission.

Gatefold, outside: Quiet envelops the field at the Gathering of the Warbirds after an intense day of activities. The Madera, California gathering usually attracts over 100 World War II aircraft, over one-quarter of which once were Mustangs. At the *far left* is a Curtiss P-40 Warhawk, with Bill DeStefani's P-51 *Strega* next to it.

Gatefold, inside: The B-17G *Sentimental Journey* visits Boeing Field in Seattle for the 1985 50th anniversary celebration of the B-17 Flying Fortress. As part of the ceremonies, 'Medal of Honor flights' were conducted, in which several World War II veterans, who had earned their Medals of Honor in B-17s, were given the opportunity to once again pilot a B-17.

Final page: A Grumman F6F-5 Hellcat restored back to its 1943 glory in 1989.